2022
ONE YEAR
PLANNER

This Book Belongs To:

....

....

PERSONAL *Information*

NAME

ADDRESS

CITY   STATE

HOME   CELL

EMAIL

COMPANY NAME

ADDRESS

CITY   STATE

PHONE   CELL

EMAIL

DOCTOR

DENTIST

ALLERGIES

BLOOD TYPE

ESSENTIAL INFORMATION

EMERGENCY

NOTIFY & RELATIONSHIPS

ADDRESS

CITY   STATE

PHONE

EMAIL

PERSONAL *Information*

NAME

ADDRESS

CITY STATE

HOME CELL

EMAIL

COMPANY NAME

ADDRESS

CITY STATE

PHONE CELL

EMAIL

DOCTOR

DENTIST

ALLERGIES

BLOOD TYPE

ESSENTIAL INFORMATION

EMERGENCY

NOTIFY & RELATIONSHIPS

ADDRESS

CITY STATE

PHONE

EMAIL

Website:

USERNAME: _____

EMAIL: _____ **PHONE:** _____

PASSWORD: _____

NOTES: _____

_____

Website:

USERNAME: _____

EMAIL: _____ **PHONE:** _____

PASSWORD: _____

NOTES: _____

_____

Website:

USERNAME: _____

EMAIL: _____ **PHONE:** _____

PASSWORD: _____

NOTES: _____

_____

Website:

USERNAME:_____

EMAIL:_____ PHONE:_____

PASSWORD:_____

NOTES:_____

_____

Website:

USERNAME:_____

EMAIL:_____ PHONE:_____

PASSWORD:_____

NOTES:_____

_____

Website:

USERNAME:_____

EMAIL:_____ PHONE:_____

PASSWORD:_____

NOTES:_____

_____

Website:

USERNAME:_____

EMAIL:_____ PHONE:_____

PASSWORD:_____

NOTES:_____

_____

Website:

USERNAME:_____

EMAIL:_____ PHONE:_____

PASSWORD:_____

NOTES:_____

_____

Website:

USERNAME:_____

EMAIL:_____ PHONE:_____

PASSWORD:_____

NOTES:_____

_____

Website:

USERNAME:_____

EMAIL:_____ PHONE:_____

PASSWORD:_____

NOTES:_____

_____

Website:

USERNAME:_____

EMAIL:_____ PHONE:_____

PASSWORD:_____

NOTES:_____

_____

Website:

USERNAME:_____

EMAIL:_____ PHONE:_____

PASSWORD:_____

NOTES:_____

_____

Website:

USERNAME:_____

EMAIL:_____ PHONE:_____

PASSWORD:_____

NOTES:_____

_____

Website:

USERNAME:_____

EMAIL:_____ PHONE:_____

PASSWORD:_____

NOTES:_____

_____

Website:

USERNAME:_____

EMAIL:_____ PHONE:_____

PASSWORD:_____

NOTES:_____

_____

Website:

USERNAME:_____

EMAIL:_____ PHONE:_____

PASSWORD:_____

NOTES:_____

_____

Website:

USERNAME:_____

EMAIL:_____ PHONE:_____

PASSWORD:_____

NOTES:_____

_____

Website:

USERNAME:_____

EMAIL:_____ PHONE:_____

PASSWORD:_____

NOTES:_____

_____

Website:

USERNAME:

EMAIL: _____ PHONE: _____

PASSWORD: _____

NOTES: _____

_____

Website:

USERNAME:

EMAIL: _____ PHONE: _____

PASSWORD: _____

NOTES: _____

_____

Website:

USERNAME:

EMAIL: _____ PHONE: _____

PASSWORD: _____

NOTES: _____

_____

Website:

USERNAME:_____

EMAIL:_____ PHONE:_____

PASSWORD:_____

NOTES:_____

_____

Website:

USERNAME:_____

EMAIL:_____ PHONE:_____

PASSWORD:_____

NOTES:_____

_____

Website:

USERNAME:_____

EMAIL:_____ PHONE:_____

PASSWORD:_____

NOTES:_____

_____

Website:

USERNAME:_____

EMAIL:_____ PHONE:_____

PASSWORD:_____

NOTES:_____

_____

Website:

USERNAME:_____

EMAIL:_____ PHONE:_____

PASSWORD:_____

NOTES:_____

_____

Website:

USERNAME:_____

EMAIL:_____ PHONE:_____

PASSWORD:_____

NOTES:_____

_____

Website:

USERNAME:_____

EMAIL:_____ PHONE:_____

PASSWORD:_____

NOTES:_____

_____

Website:

USERNAME:_____

EMAIL:_____ PHONE:_____

PASSWORD:_____

NOTES:_____

_____

Website:

USERNAME:_____

EMAIL:_____ PHONE:_____

PASSWORD:_____

NOTES:_____

_____

Contact *Information*

NAME: _____

BUSINESS: _____

WEBSITE: _____

EMAIL: _____

PHONE: _____

NAME: _____

BUSINESS: _____

WEBSITE: _____

EMAIL: _____

PHONE: _____

NAME: _____

BUSINESS: _____

WEBSITE: _____

EMAIL: _____

PHONE: _____

NAME: _____

BUSINESS: _____

WEBSITE: _____

EMAIL: _____

PHONE: _____

NAME: _____

BUSINESS: _____

WEBSITE: _____

EMAIL: _____

PHONE: _____

NAME: _____

BUSINESS: _____

WEBSITE: _____

EMAIL: _____

PHONE: _____

NAME: _____

BUSINESS: _____

WEBSITE: _____

EMAIL: _____

PHONE: _____

NAME: _____

BUSINESS: _____

WEBSITE: _____

EMAIL: _____

PHONE: _____

Contact *Information*

NAME: _____

BUSINESS: _____

WEBSITE: _____

EMAIL: _____

PHONE: _____

NAME: _____

BUSINESS: _____

WEBSITE: _____

EMAIL: _____

PHONE: _____

NAME: _____

BUSINESS: _____

WEBSITE: _____

EMAIL: _____

PHONE: _____

NAME: _____

BUSINESS: _____

WEBSITE: _____

EMAIL: _____

PHONE: _____

NAME: _____

BUSINESS: _____

WEBSITE: _____

EMAIL: _____

PHONE: _____

NAME: _____

BUSINESS: _____

WEBSITE: _____

EMAIL: _____

PHONE: _____

NAME: _____

BUSINESS: _____

WEBSITE: _____

EMAIL: _____

PHONE: _____

NAME: _____

BUSINESS: _____

WEBSITE: _____

EMAIL: _____

PHONE: _____

Contact *Information*

NAME: _____ **NAME:** _____

BUSINESS: _____ **BUSINESS:** _____

WEBSITE: _____ **WEBSITE:** _____

EMAIL: _____ **EMAIL:** _____

PHONE: _____ **PHONE:** _____

NAME: _____ **NAME:** _____

BUSINESS: _____ **BUSINESS:** _____

WEBSITE: _____ **WEBSITE:** _____

EMAIL: _____ **EMAIL:** _____

PHONE: _____ **PHONE:** _____

NAME: _____ **NAME:** _____

BUSINESS: _____ **BUSINESS:** _____

WEBSITE: _____ **WEBSITE:** _____

EMAIL: _____ **EMAIL:** _____

PHONE: _____ **PHONE:** _____

NAME: _____ **NAME:** _____

BUSINESS: _____ **BUSINESS:** _____

WEBSITE: _____ **WEBSITE:** _____

EMAIL: _____ **EMAIL:** _____

PHONE: _____ **PHONE:** _____

Contact *Information*

NAME: _____	NAME: _____
BUSINESS: _____	BUSINESS: _____
WEBSITE: _____	WEBSITE: _____
EMAIL: _____	EMAIL: _____
PHONE: _____	PHONE: _____

NAME: _____	NAME: _____
BUSINESS: _____	BUSINESS: _____
WEBSITE: _____	WEBSITE: _____
EMAIL: _____	EMAIL: _____
PHONE: _____	PHONE: _____

NAME: _____	NAME: _____
BUSINESS: _____	BUSINESS: _____
WEBSITE: _____	WEBSITE: _____
EMAIL: _____	EMAIL: _____
PHONE: _____	PHONE: _____

NAME: _____	NAME: _____
BUSINESS: _____	BUSINESS: _____
WEBSITE: _____	WEBSITE: _____
EMAIL: _____	EMAIL: _____
PHONE: _____	PHONE: _____

Contact *Information*

NAME: _____

BUSINESS: _____

WEBSITE: _____

EMAIL: _____

PHONE: _____

NAME: _____

BUSINESS: _____

WEBSITE: _____

EMAIL: _____

PHONE: _____

NAME: _____

BUSINESS: _____

WEBSITE: _____

EMAIL: _____

PHONE: _____

NAME: _____

BUSINESS: _____

WEBSITE: _____

EMAIL: _____

PHONE: _____

NAME: _____

BUSINESS: _____

WEBSITE: _____

EMAIL: _____

PHONE: _____

NAME: _____

BUSINESS: _____

WEBSITE: _____

EMAIL: _____

PHONE: _____

NAME: _____

BUSINESS: _____

WEBSITE: _____

EMAIL: _____

PHONE: _____

NAME: _____

BUSINESS: _____

WEBSITE: _____

EMAIL: _____

PHONE: _____

Contact *Information*

NAME: _____

BUSINESS: _____

WEBSITE: _____

EMAIL: _____

PHONE: _____

NAME: _____

BUSINESS: _____

WEBSITE: _____

EMAIL: _____

PHONE: _____

NAME: _____

BUSINESS: _____

WEBSITE: _____

EMAIL: _____

PHONE: _____

NAME: _____

BUSINESS: _____

WEBSITE: _____

EMAIL: _____

PHONE: _____

NAME: _____

BUSINESS: _____

WEBSITE: _____

EMAIL: _____

PHONE: _____

NAME: _____

BUSINESS: _____

WEBSITE: _____

EMAIL: _____

PHONE: _____

NAME: _____

BUSINESS: _____

WEBSITE: _____

EMAIL: _____

PHONE: _____

NAME: _____

BUSINESS: _____

WEBSITE: _____

EMAIL: _____

PHONE: _____

Contact *Information*

NAME: _____

BUSINESS: _____

WEBSITE: _____

EMAIL: _____

PHONE: _____

NAME: _____

BUSINESS: _____

WEBSITE: _____

EMAIL: _____

PHONE: _____

NAME: _____

BUSINESS: _____

WEBSITE: _____

EMAIL: _____

PHONE: _____

NAME: _____

BUSINESS: _____

WEBSITE: _____

EMAIL: _____

PHONE: _____

NAME: _____

BUSINESS: _____

WEBSITE: _____

EMAIL: _____

PHONE: _____

NAME: _____

BUSINESS: _____

WEBSITE: _____

EMAIL: _____

PHONE: _____

NAME: _____

BUSINESS: _____

WEBSITE: _____

EMAIL: _____

PHONE: _____

NAME: _____

BUSINESS: _____

WEBSITE: _____

EMAIL: _____

PHONE: _____

Contact *Information*

NAME: _____

BUSINESS: _____

WEBSITE: _____

EMAIL: _____

PHONE: _____

NAME: _____

BUSINESS: _____

WEBSITE: _____

EMAIL: _____

PHONE: _____

NAME: _____

BUSINESS: _____

WEBSITE: _____

EMAIL: _____

PHONE: _____

NAME: _____

BUSINESS: _____

WEBSITE: _____

EMAIL: _____

PHONE: _____

NAME: _____

BUSINESS: _____

WEBSITE: _____

EMAIL: _____

PHONE: _____

NAME: _____

BUSINESS: _____

WEBSITE: _____

EMAIL: _____

PHONE: _____

NAME: _____

BUSINESS: _____

WEBSITE: _____

EMAIL: _____

PHONE: _____

NAME: _____

BUSINESS: _____

WEBSITE: _____

EMAIL: _____

PHONE: _____

Contact *Information*

NAME: _____

BUSINESS: _____

WEBSITE: _____

EMAIL: _____

PHONE: _____

NAME: _____

BUSINESS: _____

WEBSITE: _____

EMAIL: _____

PHONE: _____

NAME: _____

BUSINESS: _____

WEBSITE: _____

EMAIL: _____

PHONE: _____

NAME: _____

BUSINESS: _____

WEBSITE: _____

EMAIL: _____

PHONE: _____

NAME: _____

BUSINESS: _____

WEBSITE: _____

EMAIL: _____

PHONE: _____

NAME: _____

BUSINESS: _____

WEBSITE: _____

EMAIL: _____

PHONE: _____

NAME: _____

BUSINESS: _____

WEBSITE: _____

EMAIL: _____

PHONE: _____

NAME: _____

BUSINESS: _____

WEBSITE: _____

EMAIL: _____

PHONE: _____

Contact *Information*

NAME: _____   **NAME:** _____

BUSINESS: _____   **BUSINESS:** _____

WEBSITE: _____   **WEBSITE:** _____

EMAIL: _____   **EMAIL:** _____

PHONE: _____   **PHONE:** _____

NAME: _____   **NAME:** _____

BUSINESS: _____   **BUSINESS:** _____

WEBSITE: _____   **WEBSITE:** _____

EMAIL: _____   **EMAIL:** _____

PHONE: _____   **PHONE:** _____

NAME: _____   **NAME:** _____

BUSINESS: _____   **BUSINESS:** _____

WEBSITE: _____   **WEBSITE:** _____

EMAIL: _____   **EMAIL:** _____

PHONE: _____   **PHONE:** _____

NAME: _____   **NAME:** _____

BUSINESS: _____   **BUSINESS:** _____

WEBSITE: _____   **WEBSITE:** _____

EMAIL: _____   **EMAIL:** _____

PHONE: _____   **PHONE:** _____

2022

January

MON	TUE	WED	THU	FRI	SAT	SUN
					1	2
3	4	5	6	7	8	9
10	11	12	13	14	15	16
17	18	19	20	21	22	23
24	25	26	27	28	29	30
31						

February

MON	TUE	WED	THU	FRI	SAT	SUN
	1	2	3	4	5	6
7	8	9	10	11	12	13
14	15	16	17	18	19	20
21	22	23	24	25	26	27
28						

March

MON	TUE	WED	THU	FRI	SAT	SUN
	1	2	3	4	5	6
7	8	9	10	11	12	13
14	15	16	17	18	19	20
21	22	23	24	25	26	27
28	29	30	31			

April

MON	TUE	WED	THU	FRI	SAT	SUN
				1	2	3
4	5	6	7	8	9	10
11	12	13	14	15	16	17
18	19	20	21	22	23	24
25	26	27	28	29	30	

May

MON	TUE	WED	THU	FRI	SAT	SUN
						1
2	3	4	5	6	7	8
9	10	11	12	13	14	15
16	17	18	19	20	21	22
23	24	25	26	27	28	29
30	31					

June

MON	TUE	WED	THU	FRI	SAT	SUN
		1	2	3	4	5
6	7	8	9	10	11	12
13	14	15	16	17	18	19
20	21	22	23	24	25	26
27	28	29	30			

July

MON	TUE	WED	THU	FRI	SAT	SUN
				1	2	3
4	5	6	7	8	9	10
11	12	13	14	15	16	17
18	19	20	21	22	23	24
25	26	27	28	29	30	31

August

MON	TUE	WED	THU	FRI	SAT	SUN
1	2	3	4	5	6	7
8	9	10	11	12	13	14
15	16	17	18	19	20	21
22	23	24	25	26	27	28
29	30	31				

September

MON	TUE	WED	THU	FRI	SAT	SUN
			1	2	3	4
5	6	7	8	9	10	11
12	13	14	15	16	17	18
19	20	21	22	23	24	25
26	27	28	29	30		

October

MON	TUE	WED	THU	FRI	SAT	SUN
					1	2
3	4	5	6	7	8	9
10	11	12	13	14	15	16
17	18	19	20	21	22	23
24	25	26	27	28	29	30
31						

November

MON	TUE	WED	THU	FRI	SAT	SUN
	1	2	3	4	5	6
7	8	9	10	11	12	13
14	15	16	17	18	19	20
21	22	23	24	25	26	27
28	29	30				

December

MON	TUE	WED	THU	FRI	SAT	SUN
			1	2	3	4
5	6	7	8	9	10	11
12	13	14	15	16	17	18
19	20	21	22	23	24	25
26	27	28	29	30	31	

New Year's Day	January 1
Martin Luther King Day	January 17
Presidents' Day	February 21
Memorial Day	May 30
Juneteenth	June 19
Juneteenth (observed)	June 20
Independence Day	July 4
Labor Day	September 5
Columbus Day	October 10
Veterans Day	November 11
Thanksgiving Day	November 24
Christmas Day	December 25
Christmas Day (observed)	December 26

2022

January

MON	TUE	WED	THU	FRI	SAT	SUN
					1	2
3	4	5	6	7	8	9
10	11	12	13	14	15	16
17	18	19	20	21	22	23
24	25	26	27	28	29	30
31						

February

MON	TUE	WED	THU	FRI	SAT	SUN
	1	2	3	4	5	6
7	8	9	10	11	12	13
14	15	16	17	18	19	20
21	22	23	24	25	26	27
28						

March

MON	TUE	WED	THU	FRI	SAT	SUN
	1	2	3	4	5	6
7	8	9	10	11	12	13
14	15	16	17	18	19	20
21	22	23	24	25	26	27
28	29	30	31			

April

MON	TUE	WED	THU	FRI	SAT	SUN
				1	2	3
4	5	6	7	8	9	10
11	12	13	14	15	16	17
18	19	20	21	22	23	24
25	26	27	28	29	30	

May

MON	TUE	WED	THU	FRI	SAT	SUN
						1
2	3	4	5	6	7	8
9	10	11	12	13	14	15
16	17	18	19	20	21	22
23	24	25	26	27	28	29
30	31					

June

MON	TUE	WED	THU	FRI	SAT	SUN
		1	2	3	4	5
6	7	8	9	10	11	12
13	14	15	16	17	18	19
20	21	22	23	24	25	26
27	28	29	30			

Notes

2022

July

MON	TUE	WED	THU	FRI	SAT	SUN
				1	2	3
4	5	6	7	8	9	10
11	12	13	14	15	16	17
18	19	20	21	22	23	24
25	26	27	28	29	30	31

August

MON	TUE	WED	THU	FRI	SAT	SUN
1	2	3	4	5	6	7
8	9	10	11	12	13	14
15	16	17	18	19	20	21
22	23	24	25	26	27	28
29	30	31				

September

MON	TUE	WED	THU	FRI	SAT	SUN
			1	2	3	4
5	6	7	8	9	10	11
12	13	14	15	16	17	18
19	20	21	22	23	24	25
26	27	28	29	30		

October

MON	TUE	WED	THU	FRI	SAT	SUN
					1	2
3	4	5	6	7	8	9
10	11	12	13	14	15	16
17	18	19	20	21	22	23
24	25	26	27	28	29	30
31						

November

MON	TUE	WED	THU	FRI	SAT	SUN
	1	2	3	4	5	6
7	8	9	10	11	12	13
14	15	16	17	18	19	20
21	22	23	24	25	26	27
28	29	30				

December

MON	TUE	WED	THU	FRI	SAT	SUN
			1	2	3	4
5	6	7	8	9	10	11
12	13	14	15	16	17	18
19	20	21	22	23	24	25
26	27	28	29	30	31	

Notes

YEARLY PLANNER 2022

	January	February	March	April	May	June
1						
2						
3						
4						
5						
6						
7						
8						
9						
10						
11						
12						
13						
14						
15						
16						
17						
18						
19						
20						
21						
22						
23						
24						
25						
26						
27						
28						
29						
30						
31						

YEARLY PLANNER 2022

	July	August	September	October	November	December
1						
2						
3						
4						
5						
6						
7						
8						
9						
10						
11						
12						
13						
14						
15						
16						
17						
18						
19						
20						
21						
22						
23						
24						
25						
26						
27						
28						
29						
30						
31						

January 2022

MONDAY	TUESDAY	WEDNESDAY	THURSDAY
3	4	5	6
10	11	12	13
17	18	19	20
24	25	26	27
31			

January 2022

FRIDAY	SATURDAY	SUNDAY	NOTES
		1	2
7	8	9	
14	15	16	
21	22	23	
28	29	30	

February 2022

MONDAY	TUESDAY	WEDNESDAY	THURSDAY
	1	2	3
7	8	9	10
14	15	16	17
21	22	23	24
28			

February 2022

FRIDAY	SATURDAY	SUNDAY	NOTES
4	5	6	
11	12	13	
18	19	20	
25	26	27	

March

2022

MONDAY	TUESDAY	WEDNESDAY	THURSDAY
	1	2	3
7	8	9	10
14	15	16	17
21	22	23	24
28	29	30	31

March 2022

FRIDAY	SATURDAY	SUNDAY	NOTES
4	5	6	
11	12	13	
18	19	20	
25	26	27	

April 2022

MONDAY	TUESDAY	WEDNESDAY	THURSDAY
4	5	6	7
11	12	13	14
18	19	20	21
25	26	27	28

April 2022

FRIDAY	SATURDAY	SUNDAY	NOTES
	1	2	3
8	9	10	
15	16	17	
22	23	24	
29	30		

May

2022

MONDAY	TUESDAY	WEDNESDAY	THURSDAY
2	3	4	5
9	10	11	12
16	17	18	19
23	24	25	26
30	31		

May 2022

FRIDAY	SATURDAY	SUNDAY	NOTES
		1	
6	7	8	
13	14	15	
20	21	22	
27	28	29	

June 2022

MONDAY	TUESDAY	WEDNESDAY	THURSDAY
		1	2
6	7	8	9
13	14	15	16
20	21	22	23
27	28	29	30

June 2022

FRIDAY	SATURDAY	SUNDAY	NOTES
3	4	5	
10	11	12	
17	18	19	
24	25	26	

July

2022

MONDAY	TUESDAY	WEDNESDAY	THURSDAY
4	5	6	7
11	12	13	14
18	19	20	21
25	26	27	28

July

2022

FRIDAY	SATURDAY	SUNDAY	NOTES
1	2	3	
8	9	10	
15	16	17	
22	23	24	
29	30	31	

August 2022

MONDAY	TUESDAY	WEDNESDAY	THURSDAY
1	2	3	4
8	9	10	11
15	16	17	18
22	23	24	25
29	30	31	

August 2022

FRIDAY	SATURDAY	SUNDAY	NOTES
5	6	7	
12	13	14	
19	20	21	
26	27	28	

September | 2022

MONDAY	TUESDAY	WEDNESDAY	THURSDAY
			1
5	6	7	8
12	13	14	15
19	20	21	22
26	27	28	29

September 2022

FRIDAY	SATURDAY	SUNDAY	NOTES
3	4	5	
10	11	12	
17	18	19	
24	25	26	
30			

October

2022

MONDAY	TUESDAY	WEDNESDAY	THURSDAY
3	4	5	6
10	11	12	13
17	18	19	20
24	25	26	27
31			

October 2022

FRIDAY	SATURDAY	SUNDAY	NOTES
	1	2	
7	8	9	
14	15	16	
21	22	23	
28	29	30	

November 2022

MONDAY	TUESDAY	WEDNESDAY	THURSDAY
	1	2	3
7	8	9	10
14	15	16	17
21	22	23	24
28	29	30	

November 2022

FRIDAY	SATURDAY	SUNDAY	NOTES
4	5	6	_____
11	12	13	_____
18	19	20	_____
25	26	27	_____
			_____

December 2022

MONDAY	TUESDAY	WEDNESDAY	THURSDAY
			1
5	6	7	8
12	13	14	15
19	20	21	22
26	27	28	29

December

2022

FRIDAY	SATURDAY	SUNDAY	NOTES
2	3	4	
9	10	11	
16	17	18	
23	24	25	
30	31		

Notes

Notes

Notes

Notes

Notes

Notes

Notes

Made in the USA
Columbia, SC
14 January 2022

54290277R00035